GIRLS FROM THE COUNTY

Published by Raw Dog Screaming Press
Bowie, MD
All rights reserved.
First Edition

Cover created by Steven Archer and Donna Lynch,
with contributions from Sarah Karinja
Back cover photo by Rebecca Flynn

Book design: Jennifer Barnes

Printed in the United States of America
ISBN: 9781947879478

Library of Congress Control Number:
2022934335

www.RawDogScreaming.com

GIRLS FROM THE COUNTY

poetry by
Donna Lynch

RAW DOG
SCREAMING
PRESS

Contents

Also by Donna Lynch

Author's Note

As I write this there is a giant social media storm happening over Content and Trigger Warnings in horror. I'm an unwavering believer in free will and I do not support censorship in art. Horror is personal. It should be *horrific*. What horror is should be defined by the creator and the consumer. Personally, my horror doesn't feel safe for some—not even to me, at times—but that is what makes it *my* horror.

That said, the following pages contain themes of sexual assault, addiction, suicide, mental illness, trauma, and murder, and it cost nothing but some space on a page to tell you this.

To the county girls—
Sarah, Rebecca, Julie, Lisa Marie, Alice, Ginnie, Amy,
Kristen, Kate, Carol, Jennifer, Jessica, Mickey, Jess, Lauren,
Joady, Penny, Debbie, Celia, Sara, Asia, Michelle, Zaida,
Claire, Lori Beth, M, and Erika
for always doing whatever they had to do.
And to my mother and grandmother
and all the former county girls who taught us how.

Notes from the County

I've changed the names, but these poems are true stories.

Some of them belong to me, some belong to my friends and to ghosts, and some are tapestries stitched together from all of us.

Some of the stories are from 100 years ago. Others, from thirty, and it almost doesn't matter, because certain things never change.

I grew up in rural Maryland, raised by my mother and grandmother—county girls, themselves— in the house my architect grandfather built for them in the 1940s. I lived in the house from my birth in 1974 until 1993, at which time I moved to Baltimore, got married, and started a music career that allowed my husband and I to travel—which had always been my goal. My wanderlust has been a driving force since I was fourteen years old.

We moved back to my childhood home in 2010, shortly after my beloved grandmother died.

I love our house and our woods, but there were many difficulties moving back to the county.

There are a lot of ghosts here.

The town has changed drastically since the 1990s, let alone the 1890s, becoming less rural and more suburban, but it's still recognizable in places. You could hold up an old photo against any plot of land or building and almost see it as it used to be. It's even easier to do this in your head. I still remember where things happened in my life, and the lives of my friends, even as the scenery changes. I wrote in the piece "The Exodus of Us": *We are part of this old landscape.*

If ghosts exist, perhaps this is how it happens. The marks of things that happen in a place never really go away, nor do the pieces of us we leave there.

My goal with this collection was to combine personal horror and trauma of all of the young women I knew—myself included, melancholic nostalgia, and rural legends and folklore, especially from eras before the internet, social media, and cell phones. I love technology, and don't subscribe to the whole *back in my day, things were better, we didn't have our faces in our phones* belief, so as I see it, things weren't better or worse, just different. My life was different from my mother's, hers from my grandmother's, and so on, and those differences factor into our experiences. There was an independence afforded to us, because once we left our houses, there was no tracking us down—something that was amazing and so desirable then but strikes a startling chord of anxiety in me now. I don't have children, but I would be so nervous if I couldn't reach my mother or father or husband, if need be. I can't imagine what that would feel like with a child, but I guess our parents had no basis for comparison back then. I do remember there was a lot of *call me when you get there* and hoping you didn't forget.

As children and teens, we had to make good choices out there on our own. If we didn't, there was always a window of nail-biting where you waited to see what manner of consequence would come. My first stepfather was a source of that fear in my house, but I got by because I was never inclined to make too much trouble for anyone. I was often the mom of my circle, but I watched helplessly at times (I was fairly responsible, but I wasn't a narc) as members of that circle faced a spectrum—minor to unfathomable—of consequences, sometimes of their own making, and many, many times, at the hands of others. Most made it through well enough.

Some made it through, but worse for the wear.

And some didn't make it at all.

I paint a picture in these pieces of the constant threat of predators—nearly all of which are men. This isn't because I think all men are monsters, but because the monsters that hurt us were largely male.

So, this book isn't about how men are evil.

I knew a lot of good fathers, and brothers, boyfriends, friends, bosses, and teachers. Men that knew when something wasn't okay, men who didn't struggle to make the right decision. Men who stood up for us when we couldn't do it alone.

But this book isn't about that, either.

This isn't a book that's meant to prove a point, because deep down, I believe we know who we are as a society. We know what the world looks like, and if we don't, it's because our eyes are intentionally closed.

This book is merely a record of dark events, the kind that you can sometimes move on from, yet can't help but see in every old house, high school, or crumbling bridge.

One regret I have in writing this is that growing up rural in my particular region meant I didn't have much exposure to other races and ethnicities or genders and sexualities, so there is a glaring lack of diversity in the voices in this book. But in the interest of telling the stories I experienced and heard and witnessed firsthand and not moving within lanes I'll never know how to drive in, I've written what I know. As an *adult in* this century, there's no reason for such a lack of diversity in life or art, and I will forever read and listen to the stories of people who grew up in very different worlds than I did. I'm glad I can do that now. I wish I could've known how to back then.

In the county, we were told that the city was full of monsters—something as a little kid I didn't understand to be entirely racist and classist, but I definitely caught that subtext as a teenager. We were told we could trust the adults in our community. We were told we were safe. And we went along with it even as we were lied to, even when we had early evidence to the contrary. We told ghost stories about the haunted barns and suicide cliffs at length, but never said much at all about the ghosts and demons and ugly secrets we carried with us. The demons were friends with our parents. They were family. They were our teachers and protectors, but as we all knew—bad things only *really* happen in the city. Not here.

Slowly we learned that the cursed woods or falling witch

house didn't seem as dangerous as going to the teen center or a friend's party or even going home. We all got really good at seeing the scars and ghosts we carried on our backs like we were in a secret club. I was much older before I realized the club was much bigger than any of us imagined, which is why this book isn't just about *my* county, but the counties, villages, and towns of numerous friends on two continents. These pieces exist as a record for so many young women, in so many places, who all knew each other long before ever meeting. And we still recognize each other three or four decades later.

—Signed, a county girl
Bel Air, Maryland
June 4, 2021

The Exodus of Us

It didn't matter if we stayed or ran
or ran around
and back again
We took the witches and woods
the dirt roads and devils
and the marks they left upon us
everywhere we went

We could spot each other in the wild
our dirty knees and nails
the scent of moss and feral creatures
underneath the oils and perfumes
And three long decades later
most of us have learned
that the addresses don't matter
Most of us have seen
that the exits are plentiful and clear

And it doesn't matter if we stay or run
or run around

and back again
we are part of this old landscape
just like we've always been.

These Places Want to Kill You

These fields and open spaces
will be the death of you
when you can't find your bearings
and there is nowhere left to hide

These open mouths of mines and quarries
hungry but immobile
wait quietly beyond the tree lines
for you to stumble in

These skeletons of ancient bridges
balancing on broken femurs
begging you to cross them
wanting you to break, as well

These attics and these cellars
all broken glass and nails and ghosts
tear your flesh and leave you fearful
hoarding all you wish to hide

These places want to kill you
These places want to win

These places cannot help it
These places want you dead

These places want to bleed you
These places want to feed
These places will not let you go
These places want you dead.

A New Day, Every Day

I wanted to be one of those girls
who died tragically
and full of secrets,
secrets that one
by
one
were revealed
like the days on an Advent Calendar
but behind each paper door
there was no treat
only
the names of people
I did ugly things with
and the names of people
who did ugly things
to me
But the days
have fallen
and stacked upon each other
almost comically
the way cartoons
show the passage of time

It's a new day
every day
and I'm too far beyond
the hope
that
a tragic death
could possibly
redeem
me.

Seven Minutes (i)

None of them had their Seven Minutes in Heaven
rather

28 minutes in the back of a hot, dirty car
hidden down the lane, at the far end of a graveyard

255 minutes in their best friend's brother's sleeping bag at a party
suffocating under hot, moist breath

45 indifferent minutes on a table at a clinic
where you leave through a different door than which you entered

1 ½ minutes in the swim club's humid shower room, tasting
chlorine and embarrassment, until a mom came in with her
wet-diapered kid

13 minutes, scratched and bled by briars, bitten by mosquitos,
bent over a felled tree in the woods behind the school.

Girls From the County

In Heaven (ii)

When a spacecraft approaches a celestial body
and as it enters the atmosphere
there is a moment
that the engineers call
Seven Minutes of Terror
because
it's make or break
live or die
and they hold their breath and pray they made it strong enough
to survive the landing
whole

This was how it was in those graveyard cars
and sleeping bags and showers
On paper-covered steel tables
and dead trees in humid woods
in the window of time
where it was
make or break
live or die
and you held your breath and prayed you were made strong enough
to survive those landings
whole.

Donna Lynch

Everything Was Haunted

And then
Just like that
I was a ghost
Invisible when I left the house
which could only mean
I was bound by laws
from beyond the veil
To be confined within those walls
with no one to release me
No small children for me to quietly befriend
No one to notice when I opened a door
or moved a book

And so, I was a ghost
Until I wasn't

And then I came to understand
it wasn't me
I wasn't *haunting*
but rather *haunted*
Everything was haunted
Every place I saw

Every place I went
there were warnings
and fires in my gut
and all around
lit by dead guardians
to try to tell me
when to hide
and when to run
which doors to never open
which hands to never trust

But it was too much
to suddenly be seen
when before I'd been so muted
made of tissue
made of nothing
I did not hide
I did not run

And then

because I didn't listen to the warnings

just like that

I was a ghost again.

Witch, Please

It's insulting the way
lore and legend
paint the picture
of young women
maligned
abused
run aground for witchcraft
as helpless fools
freezing to death on rocks
falling off cliffs
slipping into rivers
surrendering
when we all know
deep down
that they're still out there
in the wilderness
waiting for us to forget their names
so when they finally come
all claws and teeth
to remind us
it will be that much more
of a surprise

and that
much
sweeter.

The Other Leeds Kids

If there was one thing the Leeds girls knew for sure
it was that no one should have thirteen children
Not because of superstition
but because you'd have to be insane
Who knows at what child-count
Mother Leeds began to lose it
And anyway—
it was an entirely irrelevant query
because they were all stuck with her mess
as it often goes with daughters
And anyway—
there's really nothing to do
when your little brother
is the devil
All that meant to the Leeds girls
is that they would be rewarded
for their mundane humanity
by being forgotten—
something entirely unsurprising
illustrated by the fact
that folklore has recorded
and celebrated

the unproven existence
of a demon son
in the pine barrens
but I can't
even
give you
one sister's
goddamn
name.

Sway

There's an old tomb
just up the road
that belongs to a captain
who was denied burial at sea
but refused to be put into the dirt
So, he was given a sepulcher
where his coffin was hung
suspended inside a deep hole
And now that the stone
has started to crumble
you can peer through the cracks
and see that the
coffin has rotted away
and
—surely to his ghost's dismay—
his remains have come
to rest upon the ground
at the bottom of his canopied pit
And as bizarre
as the method of burial may be
you can't help but wonder

—as you shine a light into that vault—
how many bones
one person can possibly have.

Hexenkopf

All us rabbit girls
are gathered at the Witch's Head
waiting on the rock
waiting in the dark
waiting for the fox
to come
and do his worst

The fox
he doesn't know
it's by our firelight
and shallow breath
he's led
and not until
he finds himself
within our vicious circle
does he see our long
and yellowed teeth

Teeth not meant for biting
but for rending
and for grinding

Girls From the County

And when the blood
that's spilled
upon the rock
is dry
Round and round
we run about
the Witch's Head
until it's time

to use our teeth
again.

The Changeling
(or Bridget's Black Stockings)

Are you a witch or are you a faerie?
Or are you the wife of Michael Cleary?

These were the two
totally rational questions
asked
before *justifiably*
bashing
a woman's brains in
for wearing
dark stockings
and walking
in the woods alone.
Maybe
there was more
to the story
but
we can't
ask
Bridget—
not anymore.

Rearranging the Jewels of Jewett

The bones of the sisters
were improperly ordered
Their remains configured
like those of insects
or mythological beasts
and the people in town knew
it was the only way
to keep the girls
from rising

They broke into the caskets
and took the girls' organs
Their lungs, hearts, and livers
Stealing away like jewel thieves in the night
Their gems were too precious to leave in the dirt
inside all those sick little bodies
and it was the only way
to keep the girls
from shining

Then, in a town near to Jewett
they fed Edwin his sister

He choked on the ashes of her burned, diseased heart
and it wasn't long before they burned him up, too
Though no one would eat him
save for the pigs
But it was the only way
to keep the girls
from feeding.

My Grandmother, The Hunter

originally published in Witches (Raw Dog Screaming Press 2010)

Could it be any colder out here in the wood?
Oh, Grandmother, what shall we do?

We'll chop up the birch and slaughter a deer
Dear child, we will make it through

Could it be any darker out here in the wood?
Oh, Grandmother, how will we see?

We'll light up our torches and walk by the moon
Dear child, just follow my lead

Could they be any crueler, these ravenous wolves?
Oh, Gran, here they come for my bones!

There's no need to cry, I'll skin them alive
Dear child, you're never alone.

Parade

In the northern village
nestled within the rites of spring
a parade would come
and everyone loves a parade

Something wicked
you might assume
given the nature of
these kinds of tales
but no—
it was a celebration
of community
rebirth
and life

And that frenetic, black-faced minstrel?
Oh, he's harmless!
Mere tradition, entertainment!
Not everything is serious!

The piper, who made the children love his song?

He's come for the rats, nothing more!
Mere tradition, public service!
Not everyone is sick, you know!

The burning effigies?
An ancient ritual, just a symbol!
Mere tradition, folklore!
Not everything is hateful!

And the good folk rolled their eyes
and pursed their lips
as you asked too many questions
because
your kind was never welcome here
and the little ones were never safe
and the mob would rather see you burn
than face the ugly truths
that sing and dance
down every street

Yet they do not fear exposure
in vast, bucolic landscapes
complicit eyes have closed
and faces turned away
For their *mere traditions*
and every wicked thing that shaped them
born of poisoned minds
and hearts of fear

are right there in the open
lit by fires
bathed in sunlight.

Drag

You and your friend
Took me down to the brook
Where no one could hear us
And no one could look

Well, the water will bite
And the water will sting
But if I shut my eyes
I won't feel a thing

I will be reborn
Baptized and bled
With the rush of the water
Through my mouth and my head

And the families will talk
And the pastor will wonder
What happened the day
The brook took me under

But you and your friend
Made a pact to stay silent

If I'd just given in
If I'd just been compliant

Now you've both become men
With wives and with wealth
Your children are darling
You all have your health

But don't get me wrong
I'm doing just fine
Like this spring, I'm eternal
This river is mine

The legend's been told
But there's no need to worry
You've covered your eyes
And spun your own story

And your children still play
On the banks, skipping stones
They swim in my body
Float over my bones

But you'll feel what I felt
When I drag them all under
To my watery hell
Like when we were younger.

Identification

Way out here at night
I've learned to identify
the fox
and the bobcat
the hawks
and the owls
the sounds of mating
and sounds of fighting
so
it's unsettling
that I've yet to identify
all the other screams.

Vernal Pool

Back when I still believed
that dreams could tell you
things you didn't
already know
one of those dreams told me
that girls who never made it home
ended up in springs
and
vernal pools

The spring girls are eternal
always bleeding back into the world
but the girls of the ephemeral ponds
are a different breed
appearing only once a year
like apparitions
of virgins in waterfalls
and mountain caves

The pools are void of predators
a low and sacred place
to get a second chance

to see the girls again
and say hello
or say goodbyes you never could

But that's the beautiful thing
—or so it was in my dream—
Everything that dies
returns
and I want that to be as true
for murdered girls
as it is for frogs and salamanders

I want to see them thriving
in the springtime forest ponds
and flowing free and clean and cold
in the clear and shaded creeks
year after year
among the mosses
and the ferns
year after year
and always.

Jericho

If you listen to the rumors
and whisperings of legend
the covered bridge
has hosted hangings
since 1865

It's said
that if you stop there
high above
the cold, dark creek
some poor souls
strung from the rafters
will be swaying
in the night

All the lovers
the tormented
those who fell from crumbling towers
now the hanged men
from a bridge
made
of rotting wood

and tarot cards

It's said
that if you see them
in that right place
at that wrong time
high above the cold, dark creek
it will be you
who swings there next
as the heavy cost
that comes
with turning tragedy
to teenage games
of risk
and myth
and double dare.

Donna Lynch

It's a Mystery

I wish more people questioned why
these peaceful spaces
inhabited by decent folk
far away from the ills and sins of city life
are rife with the ghosts
of dead little kids.

When They Finally Burn You Down (Mister Rehmeyer's House)

Never trust a river witch
especially the one down in Hex Hollow
She's got nothing but coal and vengeance in her heart
and she laughed as the boys came for your mister
She knows they believe your mister has cursed them
She knows they believe curses come from a book
he's hidden inside you
And she knows if they can't find that book
They'll pull the pages from his hide
Rip the words right out of his tongue
And tear him to shreds
Even after he's dead
And set your pine bones ablaze

But what if you refuse to burn?
What if you
just
refuse
to burn?

The witch keeps on laughing

Donna Lynch

as your blistering body creaks
as the boys go down for their crimes
Cursed again
Cursed for good
But strong and whole you stood
understanding that
river witches are loyal to none but themselves
and often
not even that
and you and your mister and those boys
are just the dogs she keeps starving
she keeps you all fighting
until the death
But you remain
and remember
And if the day ever comes
when they finally burn you down
take the hollow with you
and take that fucking witch.

Knots

Our bathing suits
tied in knots and hidden
beneath the mattress
was one sure way
to keep us
from going to the creek
the day
it flooded
without warning
And ever since
there's something else
tied in knots
beneath my bones
that keeps me
from believing
in things I know I've seen
but cannot prove
and maybe that's that way it's meant to be—

I just wish I knew
who
or what
to thank.

Donna Lynch

Cannibal

Not five miles from my house
on a road that uses up a lot of deer
a man was arrested
for eating another man's heart

I don't think I would ever
could ever
do that
nor would I want it done to me
but I *do* wish
I could've known him
known his tastes
and asked him
why*

For the first time ever
I want to read
the food blogger's back story
more than I want
to read
the recipe.

Was it an exertion of power, like a rape? Was he just hungry? Did he care for the victim once? Or was he meat from day one? Had he wanted to carry him inside his gut like a trophy? Or could he think of no greater insult than reducing him to shit?

What did he think about as he chewed and swallowed? What would you think about? What would I?

It's a lot to digest.

Plot

There's nothing like an old family burial plot
way out in the woods
out on the prairies
that screams
There's someone in here that shouldn't be.

Blue Light

Oh, how we wanted the strange blue light
over by the tracks
to be something
anything at all
to prove there was more than *this*

In the neighborhood
everyone saw it and wondered
They stood on their porches
and dreamed for a minute
afraid and amazed
before going back inside
to their TVs
their arguments
their bills
and addictions
and secretly praying for it to return
It could have been something
come to destroy them
and that would've been fine
Anything at all

Donna Lynch

to prove there was more than *this*
and oh, how they dreamed for a minute.

Of Guillotines

I remember once
this older kid said
that if I ratted
if I told anyone about his cruelty
a murderer would come and take my head
Then I had a dream
that a cartoon man was coming down the road
to take the heads of everyone I loved
especially my mother
and my cat
and I was Alice
on a vast, green garden yard
bowed before
a raving queen
If I'm honest
I had it more than once
I dreamed it now and then
for years
Later, when I was awake
a little kid in Florida went missing
and on the news
they said

they couldn't find his head
I wondered if he'd ratted, too
and I knew that he'd never dream again
And somewhere in the head
still poised upon my neck
all those awful things were intertwined
Like a woven cord
connecting nightmares
Like three young, writhing serpents
or twenty-two piano wires
braided tight around my throat
But it was thick
too thick to sever
and it choked me for so long
and forty-some years later
I still dream
of Red Queens
and
guillotines.

Prediction

Just over the city line
there is a vacant lot
where grass won't grow
and once
stood the home
of a fortune teller
who lost her head
It was taken
from her body
by a now-imprisoned man
presumably
unhappy with his fortune
unhappy with how grim
his future looked
and I wonder if she knew
how prone he'd be
to self-fulfilling
prophecy.

Eighteen Years

originally published in Ladies & Other Vicious Creatures

(Raw Dog Screaming Press 2007)

We can't tell you what we saw that night
and even if we could
you'd never believe it

Eighteen years and I'm really
not sure that I do

I hear from my friend
and we talk
about life
about women
and he tells me again how Manhattan is eating him alive
And at the end of the call
he says

What was it? What did we see that night?

Eighteen years and it haunts him
He still doesn't know

But there was something there
at the edge of the woods
and it made no sense
Not then and not now

But the night was so cold
and we saw it was breathing
and we know that it saw us
breathing too

But my blood still runs cold when I drive past those woods
and when he asks me at least twice a year
what it was
still I can't tell him
and I doubt I ever will

Eighteen years, I can't say it
but I'm sure it's still there.

We Think They Murdered Andre

You can't run around making accusations without evidence,
    they said
You always want to make things more dramatic than they are
Always looking for crimes and conspiracies
Or outrageous explanations
Looking to make trouble
Do you see how upset
those poor boys are
How could they
be so upset

if

that day
at the river

it had been
anything

other
than

an
accident.

Residents

Way back in the quiet Delta woods
next to a creek
there was a house
with something in the window
Take a quick look, but don't look too long
and you hoped it was only a trick of the light
or some reflection of the trees outside
rather than something living within
and when you got closer
The longer you look, the worse it gets
you prayed it was more like a television screen
than a simple glass pane
And you prayed it wouldn't move
You prayed it wouldn't see you.

go to the last page to see

The Quarry Inside Me

I was certain
there were bodies
decomposing
bloating
melting away
inside the sunken freezers
And the cars
rusting on the quarry floor
had once been weapons
taking the lives of dogs and bikers
and distracted children
And maybe it's cliché
but there has to be a place
deep inside
to hide the corpses
the weapons
the crime
Some things
you have to sink
in the rain-filled mines
because they're just too big
to bury.

Girls From the County

Some girls from the county
shouldn't be
It is not bright enough
loud enough
high enough there
to contain them

They are the ones
who run to the cities
to deserts
to oceans
when they can no longer breathe

Some of them flourish in the wild
then pass into light
into sand
into ether
Even the ones who are left to die alone
in cars
Which is the price we pay
for raising some girls
in captivity.

Donna Lynch

Guys Like Jeffrey

He looked young
at what could've been
seventeen or twenty-five
and played guitar

I was tall
and so grown-up
at what could've been
fourteen or seventeen
going to the boardwalk
all alone

If you guessed we were as far apart as possible
you'd be correct
But we didn't get around to talking numbers
until we'd gone too far—
No
not like that—
Just conversation
and connection
and for hours I felt safe
even when he drove me home

That is
until our conversation
and connection
made us miss the road
and we drove far enough away
into another state
far enough away
for it to be a felony
and I remember
my heart dropped to my stomach
a heat rose between my legs
a hot pressure in my bladder
and I remember shaking
laughing nervously
pretending I was fine
because in the movies
when you panic
that's when
they know
you know
exactly
what
they're
gonna
do
and I can't believe
I did
the
one

thing
my mother said
to never do
and suddenly
I felt so sad
that the dashboard of his car
and the blurry dunes outside the window
might be the last thing
I'd ever see

I wished we'd both been seventeen

But when I saw
that he was shaking
shifting in his seat
the burning pressure in my guts
began to fade
Because
luckily for me
guys like Jeffrey
don't hurt young girls
Guys like Jeffrey,
sometimes they're only being nice
or maybe looking for connections
and I felt so special for it
Though he never even touched me
I'm sure I would've let him

But now that I am older

I know that guys like Jeffrey
walk a line between
protector | predator
angel | abductor
noble king | killer
and the morning could've found me
floating in the marsh
as easily
as sleeping in my bed
And I suppose I should be grateful
there are guys out there like Jeffrey
even though
the guys like Jeffrey
are why that line | exists at all.

Grave

She grew up and became a mortician
so that when he finally died
she could make sure.

Whoever It Is That's Dreaming Me, Wake Up

If she'd known
that one day
she'd have to be
everyone's beauty queen
she would've stuck her face
into the fire
right away

If she'd known
that one day
she'd have to play
whichever role
would get her home in one piece
she would've cut out her tongue
to avoid the performance

If she'd known
that one day
she'd be hated and loved
for the exact same traits

Donna Lynch

that she'd be an adornment
that she'd be a muse
a receptacle
when she was secretly just a shell
just a vehicle
and a mirror
that she'd be a dream
at least until
someone else
opened their eyes
she would've anchored herself
to the bottom of the quarry
where the world was quiet
and solely her own

Whoever it is that's dreaming me, wake up
she'd beg
again
and again

She hated that they made her beg
So, when the day came
that she finally found
her way
to the bottom of the quarry
her face charred
tongue removed
pockets filled with stones
the dreamers cried

at their loss
and made her a martyr
setting her recovered
and desiccated remains
upon a pedestal
to be worshipped
and prayed to
and used
she knew then
once again
she was forever trapped
in the greedy hearts
of the sleeping
and the dreaming.

The Business Model*

At sixteen
we—young entrepreneurs that we were—
dreamed of going into the business
of torture
since grown men were profiting greatly in the business
of terrorizing young girls
and getting away with it
because
They didn't mean anything by it
Just one too many drinks at the party
But we knew a good opportunity when we saw it
So, we thought
you keep demanding acquiescence
And we will supply the consequences

*Girls, ages 11-17, who dread cookouts, wedding receptions, holiday gatherings, group boating trips with your father's coworkers, etc. apply within.

Jane's Disappeared

originally published in Ladies & Other Vicious Creatures

She's disappeared
Jane's disappeared
But since I haven't seen her photo stapled to a telephone pole
Or in the window at the 7-11
I guess it's safe to say she's only gone from my world

I hear from a friend of a friend that she's still breathing
And that will have to be enough for me

Jane was disappearing even when I used to see her
Fading into yellowed skin and bony angles
In the company of a useless bag of flesh that I can tell
Used to be a young girl from the county
Just like Jane and I once were
And this junkie girl, this friend, whatever—
Says to me with a brittle, wasted voice
"Oh, you have wings tattooed on your back
I really wish I had some wings"
And she reaches out to touch my skin
But I pull away

so she can't touch me
with fingers that pick at
open sores
I pull away and wish her good luck in getting off the ground
with so much poison in her veins
wings or no

Since then, I'd seen Jane from time to time
At a party or in photographs
And even once or twice we've spoken
And more than once or twice I've asked her why

And she just says
"Baby you know there's always been this thing inside me
even when we were young girls in the county"
And I know she's right
There's been something tearing at her bones and at her soul
Since I've known her
She's got her feral beasts
And I've got mine
And these monsters used to chase us through the woods
Across the field
And she and I were sisters
Always running
Just escaping by a breath

And I don't know where I was when her beast caught her
I thought she was behind me when I ran across the bridge
But I hear from a friend of a friend that she's still breathing

And that will have to be enough for me
She's out there in the world
And she's still running
And that will have to be enough for me.

To Elizabeth and Regina, with regret—

I'm sorry
this is how
you became famous
How it is
that we know
your names
You deserved better
than to be
eternally left
in a vacant lot on South Norton
or
a crumbling
Bond County barn
You deserved better
than to have
the very worst day
of your
much-too-quick lives
captured and trapped
alone and exploited

always and forever
on obsolete
camera
film.

The Seven Keepers

There was the one who claimed
she was in charge
and we agreed
because she owned the space
and gave us things
half-price

There was the one who claimed
a druid lineage
but he only showed up
for the skyclad
women

There was the one
who was our friend
but brought us there less for magick
and more
for safety

There was the one who wanted
to curse her enemies
but never realized

she was the greatest
among them

There was the one who prayed
for the strength to leave
until her husband
blew his head off
in the woods

And T and I
Screaming chaos
into the void
by age seventeen
waiting for something
otherworldly
to come and mend
our damaged hearts

The seven of us
called corners
without a compass
Cast the most imperfect circles
Morton's salt
a lump of dirt
Bic lighters
cheap votive candles
chipped-up
mixing bowls
of tap water

and feathers T found
in the yard

You might be tempted
to call it wholesome
making *magick*
with what we had
But pure intentions
were no match
for the poison
that ran through us
Each, a different strain
but toxic
nonetheless
And looking back
I shudder to think
of what we made there
if we made
anything
at all.

Education

Someone ought to teach us
to be wary of the teachers
who bend and break the rules
just for sad girls
just for pretty girls
just for you

Someone ought to teach us
that no red marks
even when you're wrong
are red flags
that we are never taught to see

Someone ought to teach us
as teachers come and go
that some leave you with lessons
you could've lived without.

Donna Lynch

Submechanophobia

I hope I never find Atlantis
I could never dive in Bali or in Crete
There's a sunken cannon
in a clear blue sea
that I can't swim near
forget forgotten, submerged cities—
there's a heavy wire grid
in the muddy floor of a
Texas canyon pool
that makes my heart race
like the murky, flooded road
beneath the river
at the Conowingo Dam
There are machines and cars and freezers
at the bottom of an old blue quarry
up by the northern line
and I feel them settle
in the pit of my stomach
sinking in the tissue
and like stones in my coat pockets
they nearly drown me—

But I do not fear the water
I can handle
all that naturally occurs
way
down
deep
but I have no tolerance
for the heavy
and unwelcomed
things
that men deposit there.

Donna Lynch

At Parties

Safety in numbers
we thought
But a pack
of hungry jackals
is far, far worse
than one
And we could hear them
barking
screaming
howling
while the music played
and the drinks spilled down our dresses
and the crowd high-fived and
bared their teeth
like wild dogs
as we passed them
in the hall
Our tangled hair and bedroom haze
and reputations on parade
It was so easy
and
eventually

expected
to get torn into pieces
portioned to the pack
and devoured every weekend
the way they do
on arid plains
and wild spaces,
the way they do
at parties.

We Could Never Find the Church

It's down that old dirt road
next to the school
It was also at the end of a cul-de-sac
in another part of town
In the abandoned Methodist chapel—
the one out by all the farms
In an old house in the village
where everything is made of rocks
and built into the granite walls
And in the vacant school up on the cliff
that overlooks it
That *Satanic Church* was everywhere
And those who'd seen it
swore it was attended
by police
and clergy
housewives
and county council members
judges
teachers
doctors
the whole goddamned town, really

yet we could never
ever
find it

But maybe—
because demons
were permitted to roam freely
inhabit our towns peacefully
given full immunity
and encouraged
to always do their worst—
There was no need
for any secret church.

Lovers

Our imaginary lovers were monsters and ghosts
and we were exempt from their terror
because we saw their true nature
and loved them above and beyond their scarred faces
their gaping black mouths
their claws and hollow eyes
A strategy that did not work as well
with the ones who looked like
regular
human
boys.

The Thing About Girls with Hammers

They never *really* wanted to leave their homes
Not like that
Their bedroom walls
lined with collages
of all the things they love
carefully excised from magazines
with pink-handled scissors
The music boxes
with tiny ballerinas
filled with samples
of expensive perfumes
on perforated paper
Chanel No.5
Calvin Klein
The scent of beautiful girls
in New York and Los Angeles
London and Paris
County girls don't smell the same
no matter what they wear
But the famous name
is all that counts
and there is a deep, deep sadness

Donna Lynch

when the slips go stale and dry
and they leave those slips behind
with the other paper dreams
stuck to bedroom walls and mirrors
with scotch tape

The girls all leave for many reasons
Some of the girls are tired of yelling and fighting
Some are tired of worse
And some are just tired of cutting out pictures
of things they covet
and will never have
But these girls are tough
and by twelve
they've had to prove it
While playing video games in their parent's den with their
    brother's friends
At a playground after dark
Way down a cemetery road
In abandoned farmhouses
And factory ruins
the home of so many second-rate Satanic rituals
that only your friend's cousin's boyfriend had ever seen
These are the places they realize their strength
and by the time they take to the streets
they're not afraid of anything
except losing that job at the 7-11
that could barely cover rent

And the men can smell those empty wallets
like any predator
trailing injured prey
They have a second bedroom
They could use some help around the place
Dishes
Laundry
Nothing weird
Just convenient
And the girls all think
convenient for who?
But they pack up their clothes and drug store makeup
and stuff their red flags
into bags
from the car
They check the lock on their bedroom door
they know doesn't work
He says he's been meaning to fix it
Just a quick trip
to the hardware store
and he'll fix it
But he's already looked at them
in some kind of way
and before very long
the hammer they found
next to the dryer
down in the basement
makes its way to their room

lying
heavily
in wait
in the space
between the mattress
and the wall

You see
the thing about girls with hammers
is that they made their own choices
as they'll be the first ones to tell you
They did what they needed to do back then
and they'll do what they need to do again
maybe tomorrow
maybe next month
maybe at 4am
after everyone is asleep
creep into his bedroom
close their eyes
make a wish
and take out his jaw and his teeth
But there are moments
when they wish
wish to God
that the hammer
was a pair of pink-handled scissors
and the only thing
they ever had to destroy
was a magazine.

Girls From the County

When the Cloud Comes for You

Dorothy, who thought she could control the winds
Who thought the planets had a plan
just for her
as though she was some kind of star
wanted nothing more
than to send the storms
to ruin the lives of her tormentors

"The whole fucking town can get blown straight to hell"
she'd say, every time she drank
and nobody blamed her
we were only half-listening
while our own storms were brewing

But good witch that I am
I'd try to take her home
and tell her she had everything
she needed inside her
the whole goddamned time
and there was no need
to call those clouds
because they were certain

to devastate her heart, too
with all of those terrible swirling nightmares
of being torn through
and torn down
like the old theater ruins
razed and removed
after the last F4 came
and went

But she won't go home
she says
She won't go home
She won't stop screaming
She won't stop praying for destruction and demise
Not until they pay
and not until the storm has ripped them into pieces
and they know *exactly* why it's happening
and they are battered by tree limbs
sliced up by road signs
concussed by hail
choking on remorse for every ugly thing
they ever did to her

But that's the thing, Dorothy—

What if planets have no plan for you
and the winds aren't under your command
and none of your wreckage gets blown away
or cleansed in the process

just twisted and weakened
and filled with debris
So, when the cloud comes for you, Dorothy
where will you take shelter
since you refuse to let go,
since you refuse to go home
and there's nothing but you
and your ruin?

Sharks & Minnows

The bigger fish warned
sharks can smell when you're bleeding
and boy, they weren't lying
So quick to circle
when you've barely learned to swim
And later
they tell you
you're chumming the water
simply by being in it
And you wonder
how you can survive
with that much blood in the sea
in the creek
in the lake
in the pool
unless you learn to bite back.

King Healer

After traveling for years
King Healer went up to the mountain
to get above her pain
and give it to the sky
and warm her aching spirit in the sun

She went into the ocean
to wash away the trauma
and give it to the depths
and purify her wounded heart with salt

There, she saw the droves of healers
in robes and self-appointed titles
searching for broken hearts
and pain
and loss
and empty spaces
Promising to mend the tears
And fill the voids

Promising the world
until you could not live without them

Donna Lynch

because it was you who found them
and that you called
and lo! they answered—
when they had your sacred number
all along

But soon King Healer knew
Like so many
she'd been fooled
she closed her mouth to all their poison
and her ears to platitudes
and she purged until the acrid taste was gone

Then with her tired, salty heart
spilled upon the earth
she cleared the purest path
for the pilgrims as they flocked
for and the weary
and the lost
and let them find their way
without fallacies or fees

Like any good king would
Like any good king should.

Military Zones

Off-base
at parties
the boys would tell us
so many secret things
surely classified
surely exaggerated
surely meant to justify
all the things they didn't do
and all the things they did
But there were very tall tales
of unfathomable weapons
and toxins
mutated prisoners
humanoid creatures
and mini-Philadelphia Experiments
and they'd tell us this
with sharp drags of cigarettes
furrowed brows
furious shots
and thousand-yard stares
so we'd be apt to believe

But it was always agreed
among us who left early
that our biggest worries
were those boys
and their parties.

Thirty-two Years
(Eighteen Years Reprise)

What if
what we really saw
were all the things
we could not escape
The things that could tear us
apart
if we let them
The secrets we kept
and the fear in our guts
of going back home
of going to school
of getting lost in the woods
or worse—
being found
The hurt was too heavy to carry
too real for our hearts
So, it grew lungs
and legs
It grew teeth
and tongues

Donna Lynch

and it waited for us
in the trees
And we saw what we made
We saw what we did
We saw what could kill us
if we put down our arms
and surrendered

so, we ran

He ran to the city
She ran to the coast
and me—
I guess I've kept running
But the woods is much smaller
than I had remembered
a few thorny brambles
and willowy trees
just sparce enough
to look all the way through it
and easily see
how we got it so wrong
At eighteen years
I had a suspicion
and at thirty-two years
I'm sure that I'm right
I'm sure it still travels

directly behind us
and
I'm sure that it is
unequivocally ours.

Did I Imagine Travis?

Travis lived down by the gully
and I
up on the hill
He waited with me by the road
in the dark mornings

and rarely spoke

I was maybe seven
He was older
but not by much
His hair was always greasy
he wore a sleeveless denim jacket
even in the winter
He smoked cigarettes
and it made me nervous
afraid my gran would see the butts
and think they belonged to me

I told him once
I could see ghosts
around his second-story windows

He took a deep drag of his cigarette
Like I'd seen adults do on TV
and said
they bothered him, too

For eight months
we waited together
in the dark mornings
in silence
but for the passing cars
while the ghosts just down the hill
waited for him to come home
each afternoon

The next September
he was gone

I was waiting on the dark road
in the morning
all alone
there was nothing left
in his house
not his mother
not his noisy dog
not his bike
and the records I only guessed he had
not even his ghosts remained
there was nothing to see

Donna Lynch

in the second-story windows
but the reflections
of passing cars
and no one else remembers him
so I may never know
if he was like me
or like them
but either way
I hope he isn't bothered anymore.

The Wych Elm, Hollywood, & Other Places Where They Went Asking

When small town girls go to the city
Some will be cut in half and left in vacant lots

When small town girls go out at night
Some will be slit open and robbed of their organs

When small town girls run away
Some will become nothing but a terrible, famous Polaroid

When small town girls walk drunk in the woods
Some will be folded up and left in a hollow tree

But that's the risk small town girls take
When they go outside
When they go looking
When they go asking

They go asking.

You Were So Close

Get in the car
I'm not going to hurt you
I—a grown man
just need
You—a young girl
to help me
Please help me
Turn the key
while I stand here
and study the engine
and scry into the metal
and see the future
and see what I will do
What will I do?
Just get in the car
We can find out together
And I see you hesitate
because in your twelve years
someone taught you to listen
taught you politeness
taught you to help
But you were just close enough for

Me—a grown man
to know that
You—a young girl
were going to run
And you did
And now
we'll never know
what our futures
long or short
held for us.

Acknowledgments

In addition to the women I know who inspired, contributed to, and gave me feedback on this book, I want to express my deepest gratitude to Jennifer Barnes and John Edward Lawson of Raw Dog Screaming Press, my co-editor (along with Jennifer Barnes) and unofficial advisor Stephanie M Wytovich, publicist Erin Sweet Al-Mehairi, Rebecca Flynn for the interior and back cover photographs, Steven Archer for the cover design (and his unending love and encouragement) and Sarah E Karinja for her contribution to the cover, my mom, my dads, and mother-in-law—who support my work even when it upsets them, and my dearest friends who are never too busy to listen, and all of the readers who continue to make it possible for me to do this.

Thank you.

About the Author

Donna Lynch is a two-time Bram Stoker Award-nominated dark fiction poet and author, spoken word artist, and the co-founder—along with her husband, artist and musician Steven Archer—of the dark electronic rock band Ego Likeness.

An active member of the Horror Writers Association and contributor to the *HWA Poetry Showcase*, her published works include the novels *Isabel Burning*, and *Red Horses*; the novella *Driving Through the Desert*; and the poetry collections *In My Mouth*, *Twenty-Six*, *Ladies & Other Vicious Creatures*, *The Book of Keys*, *Daughters of Lilith*, *Witches*, and the Ladies of Horror Fiction Award-winning *Choking Back the Devil*.

CPSIA information can be obtained
at www.ICGtesting.com
Printed in the USA
JSHW032116170722
28167JS00005B/234